praise
Learning
When You Fe   ...ying
Embracing Life After Loss
by Allen Klein

"This book is a wonderful companion in your darkest hours. It feels like a warm, nourishing hug from a dear and loving friend. It will soothe your heart and warm your soul. It will help you to find that sacred place within you that is never lost and never changes — your spiritual heart, your soul, which can be gracefully awakened through the mystical, transformational, holy experience of laughter."
–John E. Welshons, author of *When Prayers Aren't Answered*

"Like a dear friend, this beautiful book takes us by the hand and walks us through the stages of loss and recovery. Allen Klein has inspired us all to define ourselves, not by our grief, but by our joy."
–Susan Sparks, Pastor and author of *Laugh Your Way to Grace*

"This is an easy-to-read, compassionate, and useful book for dealing with loss and grief. Allen Klein addresses different aspects of the grieving process, all of which speak to the heart of what it is to deal with and recover from loss. This is a wonderful addition to the current literature on grief, and would make a wonderful condolence gift."
—Judy Tatelbaum, author of *The Courage to Grieve*

"Raising Lazarus from the dead is less miraculous than raising ourselves from the loss of a loved one. Allen Klein, invoking his decades of experience 'lightening the load of grief' offers an unexpected grace, a slight levitation of the heart, into the healing process."
—Stephen Levine, author of *A Year to Live*

"With great love and humor, Allen Klein shares his wisdom — wisdom that shows us the path to healing the wounds uncovered by our grief; wisdom that he has clearly earned through his own deep practice. He walks the walk. We are all grieving. Allen shows us the way, as Rumi says, to use grief as 'the garden of compassion.'"
—Dale Borglum, Executive Director of the Living/Dying Project

"Allen Klein has just written the handbook on how to cope with suffering. This book has all the tools you need to bounce back from loss of any kind."
–Steve Rizzo, author of *Becoming a Humor Being*

"Allen Klein has such a beautiful perspective! His book is an important, authentic, and liberating look on how we can move through loss with compassion, humor, and peace. If you're dealing with a loss of any kind, this book will support you in your journey."
–Mike Robbins, author of *Be Yourself, Everyone Else is Already Taken*

"Allen Klein is a counselor, a philosopher, a theologian. His pain, from losing his young wife, and his healing, from moving beyond her death, are evident in every word he writes. In easy-to-take doses, he offers practical advice on seeing the light in the darkest of times. He shares the secret that survivors — of everything from cancer to the Holocaust — have learned."
–Steve Lipman, author of *Laughter in Hell*

"There are very few books that everyone can identify with and benefit from. This is one of those books. We've all experienced a loss that leaves us dispirited and adrift. *Learning to Laugh When You Feel Like Crying: Embracing Life After Loss* recognizes that even on hallowed ground, we lose our footing and our bearings. Allen Klein encourages us to find our way and teaches us the five 'stages of living' after loss, so that we can not only survive, but thrive, enjoy, and embrace our lives."
—Alan Gettis, author of *It's All Part of the Dance: Finding Happiness in an Upside Down World*

"Klein's lucid writings make compelling connections with psychology, religion, history, philosophy, and good ol' common sense. His personal experiences, clinical examples, and delightful humor is like viewing a trapeze artist who lets go of one rope and gracefully takes hold of another, without a misstep. This is a penetrating treasure trove of profound insights and skillfully blended and constructed tools."
—Earl A. Grollman, author of *Living When a Loved One Has Died*

LEARNING TO
LAUGH
WHEN YOU FEEL LIKE
CRYING

Embracing Life After Loss

ALLEN KLEIN

Foreword by Earl A. Grollman, author of
Living When a Loved One Has Died

GOODMAN BECK PUBLISHING

GOODMAN BECK PUBLISHING

PO Box 253
Norwood, NJ 07648
www.goodmanbeck.com

Lyrics from the song "You're There," lyric by Alix Korey, music by David Friedman,
©MIDDER Music Publishing, Inc. Used by permission. All rights reserved.

ISBN 978-0-9798755-8-8

Library of Congress Control Number: 2010942317

Printed in the United States of America

10 9 8 7 6 5 4 3 2

To hospices everywhere,
who do incredible work with the dying,
the grieving, and their families.

contents

learning   *37*

Step Three
letting go   83

Step Four
living   *107*

Step Five
laughing   *155*

Foreword

In this most helpful book, Allen Klein shows how to transform your attitude toward loss—whether it be a loved one's death, the loss of a job, or the trials associated with aging—in order to return to living life more fully again.

As a pioneer in the field of loss and crisis intervention, I have seen many ways that people cope with grief and loss. Sometimes laughing is a healing medicine. The eminent psychiatrist Viktor Frankl, a concentration camp survivor, provides perhaps a most powerful example. Every day he found something funny to laugh about. He credited his survival, in part, to humor. It gave him hope to look forward to each day. It afforded him the power to rise above an almost powerless situation. I say "almost" because Frankl attributed his survival to attitude, the real power one has over any situation.

Klein is no stranger to the value of therapeutic humor as an attitude-changing tool. From his experience as a former home health aide and hospice volunteer, as well as from the personal and career losses in his life, he has amassed a wealth of compassionate wisdom. This knowledge is presented here in a very easy-to-digest, helpful, and reader-friendly format.

Like Elizabeth Kubler Ross's five stages of dying, Klein has created what he calls "the five stages of living" after loss. They are: Losing, Learning, Letting Go, Living, and Laughing.

In one of his previous books, *The Courage to Laugh: Humor, Hope, and Healing in the Face of Death and Dying*, Klein imparted encouraging stories of how those who were facing life-threatening challenges — from such crises as cancer, AIDS, lingering loss, or sudden loss — had used humor as a meaningful coping tool. In the book *Learning to Laugh When You Feel Like Crying*, Klein goes a step further. With inspirational quotations, lessons from diverse cultures, and heartwarming advice, he provides numerous suggestions for finding humor during those not-so-funny times.

While death, dying, and loss are no laughing matter, those who find a bit of humor in the grieving process know that they will survive. When laughing, you have a moment's respite in what is often an overwhelming circumstance. It is a wonderful way to communicate at a time when communication is often at an impasse. In addition, you gain a different perspective at a difficult time and rise above life's adversities.

And, perhaps the most important gain is that humor and laughter, as Frankl discovered, fosters hope. I have always been intrigued with the power that hope provides during a crisis. Without hope, all is lost.

There are many books about coping with grief and loss. I have written a few of them myself. But *Learning to Laugh When You Feel Like Crying* is unique because of its focus on enduring losses, learning from them, and beginning to live and laugh again.

I hope that you will read this book, for it will not only provide you with hope but also with a passion for life.

—Rabbi Earl A. Grollman, DHL, DD, author of
Living When a Loved One Has Died

*I always try to balance the light
with the heavy; a few tears of human
spirit, in with the sequins and the fringes.*
–Bette Midler, American entertainer

dear reader

While this book comes out of the lessons I've learned about loss from the death of my wife, the thoughts within address all kinds of loss. The feelings that often accompany the loss of a loved one also apply to such things as losing a pet, getting a divorce, being let go from a job, or any other major setback in your life. Any loss can be overwhelming. The aim of this book is to help you realize that loss is part of life, that it can be one of our greatest teachers, and that, in spite of your loss, you can once again fully partake in what life has to offer

When my wife died at the age of 34, I didn't need a book that tried to explain the complexities of grief. I didn't need a book that spoke to my head. I needed a book that would offer a few comforting words and speak to my heart.

That is what I hope this book will do for you.

With simple words and simple — yet profound — ideas, I hope that it will provide comforting, heartfelt thoughts and a lighter tone not found in other books on loss. I also hope that it will show you that there can be a positive side to loss and help you understand that, although your loss is a life-changing experience, it need not necessarily be a negative one. And that, because of life's brevity, a loss can be a powerful wake-up call to celebrate life.

Please note that I am not advocating avoiding the grief caused by loss or rushing through it. Unexpressed grief can come back again with a stronger force. It is important to fully deal with the grieving process after a loss. However, my intention in writing this book is to help you go beyond your loss to embracing life fully again and, yes, even laughing again. And to help you go from merely surviving to thriving. Also, I hope that it will uplift your spirit, touch your heart, and nourish your soul.

P.S. The advice in this book is what worked for me during my time of loss. Some of it may seem right for you, some of it may not. As with any information, take what fits and leave the rest behind.

opening diary

Sunday, June 24

I *have no sisters. I do, however, have a cousin who has been like a sister to me. We grew up together, shared many a happy moment at a Broadway show, and enjoyed numerous fun-filled meals together. And even though she lived on the East coast and I on the West, we were very close.*

Three days ago, I found out that she has leukemia. And, at her age of 78, the doctor doesn't think the prognosis is very good.

I am very upset. I have not only felt like crying in the past few days but have actually done so several times. And while I haven't consciously tried to find some humor in the situation (I am still in shock), there is a picture hanging on my wall in the hallway that brings a small smile to my face every time I see it.

It is of Bernice and some Disney-like character. The oversized bird's bright yellow beak and Bernice's nose are touching. Her face is glowing with laughter and joy.

This photo is the essence of Bernice's spirit—upbeat and playful. It is a wonderful reminder to me that although Bernice's body may be going through turmoil right now, her bright spirit will remain forever.

Wednesday, July 4

Thoughts of Bernice are all-consuming. I wake up at night thinking of her. Every time the phone rings, my fear is that there is some bad news.

Wednesday, July 11

I'm out of town attending a week-long conference in San Diego, California. The phone in my hotel room rings at two-thirty in the morning. Without even answering it, I know exactly what has happened. I check out of the hotel and I'm on plane to New York to arrange for the funeral and Bernice's burial.

Friday, July 13

Bernice's coffin is lowered into the ground. It is Friday the 13th.

Saturday, July 14

The day after the funeral, my daughter and I decide we need some quiet time together. We stay around Bernice's apartment going through some of her possessions. In the afternoon, we take advantage of the unusually cool-for-New-York summer weather and go to a nearby museum. There we spend time reflecting in a tranquil setting.

But the tranquility doesn't last long. Unbeknownst to us, it is the museum's annual fundraiser. When we enter the museum's courtyard, hundreds of people are starting to gather. The DJ is working his musical magic, the band is getting ready to take over, and the crowd is anticipating the loud and lively late afternoon.

We get caught up in the festive scene, order a beer, and delight in watching the spectacle of the young New York art scene. There we sit, forgetting — at least for a while — that Bernice's funeral occurred just a little over 24 hours before.

We also realize that the solitude we planned for that day was not to be. When the loud music gets a bit much for us, and the crowd starts to become overbearing, we head for one of Bernice's favorite neighborhood restaurants. Just before our meal arrives, a young man takes a seat next to our table. With his guitar, he plays and sings songs by the Beatles, Paul Simon, and others. He invites us to sing with him. We do. Like the museum experience, the quiet dinner we anticipated did not happen.

But what did happen was spontaneous magic. Throughout the day, it was as if Bernice's luminous spirit was saying to us, "You've cried enough. You've mourned enough. Now it's time to partake in the music of life."

Sunday, July 15

I *think of two things Bernice told me. One she shared several months prior to her death. She said that she lived her life by what her mother taught her — to bring joy to at least one person each day.*

The other thing she told me occurred when I was a teenager. It was about her world excursions. She was the first person I knew who traveled by airplane. I used to stand on LaGuardia's observation deck at the airport and waive to her as her plane took off. One day, I asked her if she was afraid that the plane might crash.

She said she wasn't, but that if it did, she would want it to be on the return flight so that she would not miss a moment of her vacation. That was Bernice — never missing a moment of what life had to offer.

Thursday, Friday, Saturday...July, August, September... and the rest of the days.

I *think of Bernice often, and with the music of her joyous spirit to guide me, I get on with life.*

Step One
losing

If you believe yourself unfortunate,
because you have loved and lost,
perish the thought. One who has
loved truly, can never lose entirely.
—Napoleon Hill, American author

Losing a loved one is not easy. I know — I have had many losses in my life. The one that made the most impact on my life was my wife's death when she was 34. In addition, my mother, my father, my four grandparents, my sister-in-law, several cousins, and both my mother-in-law and father-in-law have died, as well as over 40 friends and colleagues who are no longer here because of AIDS or cancer.

I don't think we ever forget the people we lose. So in some sense, they are never gone. But, still, it hurts not to be able to see them, hear them, or hold them again.

Loss hurts. But it can also help us be stronger, wiser, and, if nothing else, more appreciative of every moment we have on this earth.

in shock

If you're going through hell, keep going.
—Winston Churchill, British politician

When a loss occurs, shock sets in. This is natural. At the time, it may feel like you can't deal with life. That is *okay...* for now.

You may feel numb and listless.
You may not want to eat or even get out of bed in the morning.
You may feel overwhelmed.
You may feel that your life has stalled or stopped.
You may also feel angry, depressed, and even guilty.

Know that you are not going crazy. All of these are normal responses in the grief process.

why me?

*I don't know why babies are born with AIDS, young
people get killed in tragic accidents, or the Cubs
can't win a World Series. But I do believe there are
blessings in every challenge, and lessons, growth
and ultimately prosperity in what they bring us.*
        —Randy Gage, American prosperity teacher

After experiencing a loss, you may be asking yourself,
"Why has this happened to me?"

The answer to the "why me" question is twofold. First,
perhaps there is no answer to that question. And second,
you are too close to your loss right now to know the answer. While these answers don't provide much comfort,
some solace might be had knowing that we are all a small
part of a much grander universe and that, with time, your
loss will take its proper place.

Perhaps, too, the better question (or questions) to ask after a loss might be:

"How will this help me live more fully knowing that my time is limited too?"

"How will this help me contribute to the greater good for all people?"

"How will this make me become a more loving person?"

rising above your loss

*What is extraordinary about us is that we each
have the capacity to rise like the phoenix out of
our ashes, to create ourselves newly, to begin
again. We can transform ourselves and our lives,
regardless of what we have endured before now.
Maybe the true purpose of suffering is that out of
our pain, we will rise, expand, grow and achieve.*
—Judy Tatelbaum, American author/therapist

Go ahead. Wallow in your loss. It is *okay*. You probably
need that right now. But that is now, not forever. Somewhere down the road, your tears will subside.

When we experience a loss, we can focus on the tears
and on what we no longer have or we can appreciate what
we still have. We can focus on a life cut short or celebrate
a life lived. We can feel sorry for ourselves or see our loss

in a larger context.

You can get lost in your loss; you also have the power to rise above it.

During loss, it seems that you can't possibly go on. Everything in your life may seem like it has come to a standstill. But you can go on, and will go on.

the big picture

*The next time you are feeling bored, despondent
or irritable, try to remember your cosmic situation;
at this moment you are riding on a big round-shaped
rock that is hurling through space, spinning around
its own axis at about a thousand miles per hour and
spinning around the sun at approximately 66,000
miles per hour. Along with our entire solar system,
you are also soaring through the Milky Way galaxy
at nearly 500,000 miles per hour. And what's truly
remarkable is that you don't even have to hold on.*
—Wes "Scoop" Nisker, Buddhist teacher

I recently went to the planetarium in San Francisco. I saw
an incredible astronomical show about the creation of our
sun. I learned that the sun is actually a star and that it is
the nearest star to earth. I also learned that it was created

4.6 billion years ago. And it will burn itself out in another five billion years.

Fascinating numbers, but I could not wrap my mind around them. They were talking about billions of years ago and billions of years into the future. I couldn't even imagine what one million years would look like, let alone billions.

It made me realize what a small speck we are in the history of our vast universe. And how trivial some of the things we concern ourselves about really are. It also helped put my losses, which seem so overwhelming at the time, in perspective.

You may feel that your loss is the largest thing in the universe. In time, and with perspective, your loss will take its proper place in your life.

triumphing over tragedy

*The soul would have no
rainbow had the eyes no tears.*
—John Vance Cheney, American poet

Life can be filled with joy. It can also be filled with immense sadness. Our ups and downs during life's journey depend on a number of factors. These include such things as our circumstance, our reaction to our circumstance, and yes, even luck. Often we can't control our circumstance, or our luck, but we can control our reactions to what happens to us and, by doing so, overcome them.

There have been numerous books, articles, and movies about people who have risen above the difficulties that life has handed them. They have won gold medals running races with no legs, they have gone from the bottom of the heap to the top of the boardroom, and they have been devastated by the loss of a loved one. Many of them have gone on to inspire others or create organizations—like Mothers Against Drunk Drivers—to fight against the injustice that caused their loss. They have all triumphed over tragedy.

These are no super heroes. These are ordinary people who realized that they may be down but they didn't have to stay there. They too have had feel-like-crying moments, perhaps many of them. But they didn't let those times dictate their future. They eventually took those setbacks and, at some point, realized that they could surmount them.

If those people can do it, you can too.

endings are also beginnings

The world is round and the place
which may seem like the end
may also be only the beginning.
   —Ivy Baker Priest, American politician

You can't turn back the clock and undo your loss. But you can move forward by realizing that when one door closes, another opens.

After my wife died, I had no idea where my life would lead me. I knew that my world had changed, but I didn't know where it was headed. What I did know was that I had to trust the process.

The death of my wife led me first to hospice work and then to the investigation and teaching of the therapeutic value of humor. It wasn't a journey I signed up for, understood, or wanted, but, looking back, it showed me that out of death comes new life. And those setbacks often become stepping stones.

Your loss is a milestone that has made a major impact on your life. It has ended a world you once knew. But, at the same time, it has created new opportunities and an opening for the beginning of a yet-to-be-discovered world.

death is part of life

To everything there is a season,
and a time to every purpose under heaven:
A time to be born, and a time to die.
—Ecclesiastes 3:1-8, Old Testament

Everything that lives also dies. If you are reading this book, you are alive. And if you are alive, someday you will die. While we may want it to be otherwise, that is the nature of all beings. Death is not something separate from life; it is a part of it.

You might think that, in a perfect world, no one would die. That may seem like an ideal situation, but it is just the opposite.

Imagine, for a moment, a world where no one dies. It would be chaotic and unlivable. If no one died, there would not be enough places for people to live. There would not be enough food. There would not be enough jobs. There would not be enough natural resources to support humanity. And, would anything ever get accomplished knowing that there was an unending amount of time to get things done? Would people even value life knowing that it went on forever?

So, although death brings grief, it is a necessary evil. In fact, on some level, death is nature's way of keeping the world in balance.

Loss is also necessary to help us grow spiritually. Yes, loss hurts, but it can also help us be stronger, wiser, more compassionate, and if nothing else, more appreciative of every moment we have on this earth. And, while nothing can bring back your loved one, knowing that the loss is part of a vast universal truth may bring some comfort.

the hero's journey

*A hero is an ordinary individual
who finds the strength to persevere and
endure in spite of overwhelming obstacles.*
—Christopher Reeve, American actor

Joseph Campbell, the American mythologist, says that part of the human experience involves suffering certain losses, leaving our predictable comforts, and setting out into unfamiliar terrain. Inevitably, we meet with things that block our way and take us into dark places to do battle with unseen forces. Out of these struggles, we emerge with wisdom. Campbell is talking about the "hero's journey."

After a loss, you are on a hero's journey. You are in unfamiliar territory and in an uncomfortable place. You have come to a major challenge in your life and a very dark place. You are battling unfamiliar forces, and as in the he-

ro's journey, you will emerge with greater wisdom.
   It may not seem like it right now, but you too are a hero.

ask the horse

*Life is what happens to us
while we are making other plans.*
–Allen Saunders, American writer/cartoonist

There is an old Zen story about a man who was riding a galloping horse. Seeing him whizzing by, a woman shouts to the man, "Where are you going in such a hurry?" The man yells back, "I have no idea. Ask the horse!"

Most of us go through life making plans for the future despite the fact that none of us really know what the future will bring.

For many years, my wife and I wanted to live in San Francisco. My wife was from there. We would visit her parents at least once, sometimes twice, a year. We would come back home from our trips and I would draw pictures of Victorian houses. Someday, I thought, we would own one of them.

After there was a fire in our New York City apartment building, we decided to move to San Francisco — the city of our dreams. A few years after that, we bought a Victorian house that was built in 1876. Then we found out that my wife had a rare life-challenging liver disease. There were no liver transplants at the time and there was nothing that could be done for her. She died three years after the diagnosis.

That wasn't in our plans. We were supposed to live happily ever after in the house we always wanted in the City-by-the-Bay. But it was not to be. I was riding the horse in the direction I wanted to go, but the horse was going in a different direction.

Right now you may feel that what has happened to you is the worst thing in the world. But that is because you can only see the present moment. Be patient. Down the road, you will see where the horse is headed.

one step at a time

One step at a time is good walking.
−Chinese proverb

I have always been dubious when I read that some entertainer is supposedly an overnight sensation. How absurd; there are no overnight sensations. What we often learn when we dig deeper is that those performers spent years practicing their craft, performing in numerous small venues around the country, or took years of classes in order to practice and perfect their skills.

Like performers learning their craft, you are learning how to live with your loss. Things take time. Your grief won't disappear just because you want it to. In fact, it may come and go for a long time. That is its natural process.

your unique grief

I measure every Grief I meet
With narrow, probing, Eyes –
I wonder if It weighs like Mine –
Or has an Easier size.
                    –Emily Dickinson, American poet

Sometimes the biggest obstacle in getting through a loss is not the loss itself but our notion of how we should react to it. We feel that we should be sad; we should feel remorse; we should be upset. In truth, there is no right or wrong way to deal with loss, nor how long the mourning period should last, nor what stages of the grieving process we will or will not experience.

Some people think that grief lasts a year. They wonder why they are still grieving after that time. Grief has its own timetable. Just as one person is totally different from another, so too is one person's grieving process different from anyone else's.

The same is true of the intensity of grief. Some people experience a loss and move on shortly after it. For others, it takes a much longer time.

And, even though such things as anger, depression, guilt, numbness, being overwhelmed, and shock are part of grief, you may experience all of them, some of them, or none of them.

Try not to compare your grief to someone else's. You are unique.

So is your grief.

when you least expect them

Tears are the safety valve of the heart
when too much pressure is laid on it.
                              —attributed to Albert Smith

Some days, after my wife died, I would wake up in the morning feeling pretty good. I thought my tears were over. Then they would start again when I least expected it.

For example, on my way to work some days, whenever I walked past the Bank of America building in downtown San Francisco, I would burst out crying. I don't know why I did. I just did. I had no idea why it happened at that particular spot. Was it the massiveness and the darkness of the structure? I will never know.

What I do know is that grief, and the tears that it can trigger, can rear its head at the most unusual moment. Tears are a natural part of the grieving process, but you can't plan when they will happen. They seem to have a mind of their own. They might start while dining in a restaurant with friends, during a meeting at work, or while traveling on public transportation.

Don't hold back the tears. Let them flow.

setbacks are normal

All the world is full of suffering.
It is also full of overcoming.
    −Helen Keller, deaf/blind American author

What I found after my wife died was that setbacks were part of the normal grieving and healing process. Some days I would feel like I had finally put my loss behind me. Other days the loss seemed overwhelming.

You too may feel that on some days, you have taken one step forward and two backwards. Accept those days. It may not seem so now, but down the road, there is a good chance that you will take three steps forward and none back.

Your world right now may feel like it is filled with suffering. What you may not be able to see right now is that it can also be filled with overcoming.

you are not alone

*One word or a pleasing smile
is often enough to raise up a
saddened and wounded soul.*
        —Therese of Lisieux, Catholic saint

When I was about seven years old, my parents took me
to see the musical *Carousel* on Broadway. I still remember
one haunting song in that show. It is "You'll Never Walk
Alone." In the show, the song is sung to give Julie Jordan,
one of the leading characters, strength and courage after
the father of her child, Billy Bigelow, is killed.

The lyrics talk about holding your head up high, not
being afraid of the dark, and finding a golden sky at the
end of the storm. They gave me comfort and courage during many difficult times in my life. It may do the same for
you. Seek it out and listen to it, if you can. Or, find anoth-

er song, poem, quotation, book, prayer, or grief support group to remind you that you are not alone in your loss.

It may feel like you are the only one to ever experience such an intense loss, but you are not. Others have gotten through their loss and they have survived. You can too.

pat yourself on the back

Whenever you feel uncomfortable,
instead of retreating back into your
old comfort zone, pat yourself on the
back and say, "I must be growing,"
and continue moving forward.
  −T. Harv Eker, motivational speaker/author

 W hen we accidentally stub our toe or nick one of our fingers, we often shout out, "Ouch!" Grieving is the body's way of saying "ouch" after a loss. It is telling us to stop what we are doing, take some time off, and admit that loss hurts.

Dealing with a loss is not easy. You have been going through a lot. In fact, it might be the hardest thing you have ever done in your life. Perhaps it is time to acknowledge that under the circumstance, you are doing the best you can right now.

So, reach one arm over your shoulder and give yourself a great big pat on the back.

additional thoughts on losing

Should you shield the canyons from
the windstorms, you would never
see the true beauty of their carvings
—Elisabeth Kübler-Ross, Swiss-born psychiatrist

We must embrace pain and
burn it as fuel for our journey.
—Kenji Miyazawa, Japanese poet

The lights of stars that were extinguished
ages ago still reach us. So it is with great
men who died centuries ago, but still reach
us with the radiation of their personalities.
—Kahlil Gibran, poet

Step Two
learning

Turn your wounds into wisdom.
    –Oprah Winfrey, American television host

Every time you lose something, you are presented with an opportunity to acquire something new. With each loss, there is a golden opportunity for a new beginning. You may not realize it right now, but your loss is part of your growth process. In fact, your loss can be seen as a gift.

How could you possibly even think of loss as a gift? You have lost someone who was very dear to you. You have perhaps lost the one person in your life who meant everything to you. You have lost a significant part of who you were. It certainly doesn't feel like a gift.

And yet, it is.

Your loss is serving you. It is helping you examine who you are, why you are on this earth, and how to live your life. Among other things, your loss has given you:

–the gift of appreciating life more fully
–the gift of cleansing through mourning
–the gift of love

The best thing you can do after reading this is to open the gift.

the seasons

In the depth of winter, I finally
learned that within me there
lay an invincible summer.
            —Albert Camus, French writer

You may feel that you are in the midst of the coldest, darkest winter of your life. But think of the seasons. In nature, after winter comes spring and then summer always follows.

You too are part of nature. Your loss has created the season of winter. But somewhere inside of you there is also the new growth of spring and the warmth of summer waiting to emerge.

inner strength

I...walked for miles at night along the beach,
writing bad blank verse and searching endlessly
for someone wonderful who would...change my life.
It never crossed my mind that that person could be me.
                    —Anna Quindlen, American author

I am male.
I am 72 years old.
I am bald.
I have a beard.
I grew up in the Bronx.
I now live in San Francisco.
I am married.
I have one daughter.
I have one brother.
I like herbal tea, poppy seed strudel,
and kosher pickles.

I have a Master's degree.
I am a professional speaker.
I am an author.

The above list tells you a little about me. But it doesn't really tell you one of the most important things. It doesn't tell you that I am a survivor. It doesn't tell you that I have survived many losses in my life.

None of those losses, however, make me unique. We are all survivors, including you. There is a good chance that if you are alive, you have experienced the loss of people you knew or someone you loved.

Losing is part of living.
It is also part of learning.
Losing teaches you that life goes on and that you can too.

Each loss also teaches you about your inner strengths that you probably never knew you had. Now is the time to tap into them.

take courage

Pain nourishes courage.
You can't be brave if
you've only had wonderful
things happen to you.
—Mary Tyler Moore, American actress

Life is filled with trials and tribulations. They are often painful and unwanted. There is no way of avoiding them.

Still, as annoying and agonizing as they are, without those ordeals, your life would be shallow. They help mold you into who you are and bolster your courage. They help you grow as a person and increase your compassion for others who might also be in pain.

In loss, you also learn that if you can overcome your present ordeal, you have the courage within you to survive future losses as well.

remembering those who left us

*Think about someone who you've lost
and write down the ways that person
positively affected your life. How is your
life better today for having known him or her?*
—Julie Clark Robinson, American author

If you have lost a loved one or a close friend, the hardest time in the grieving process is often around the holidays. And although it may be a bitter time without them, you can sweeten those times with their loving memories.

A few things you can do, holidays or not, are:

—Recall a good-time story about them. Tell it to others.
—Cook one of their favorite foods. Share it with friends.
—Go through photo albums. Display a couple of your favorites.

43

In addition, think about how your loved ones would want you to remember them. Would they want you to be somber and solemn for the rest of your life, or would they want you to celebrate their lives by remembering the happier times you spent together?

For most of us, it would be to honor the latter.

still here

*If you're connected to someone in a moment
of love, the essence of that person is right
there with you even after their death.*
  —Ram Dass, spiritual teacher

Shortly after my wife died, I tapped into her great sense
of humor and started to do workshops on the therapeutic
value of humor and laughter. In one of my very first presentations, I was shocked when I looked around the room.
There, in the back row, was a woman who looked exactly
like my deceased wife. I was taken aback and made a mental note to speak to her at the break. When the break came,
I started to make my way to the corner where the woman
was seated, but someone interrupted me to ask a question.
By the time I got to the rear of the room, the woman was
gone. And she never returned for the second half of the

program. Was that woman really there? Was I only imagining it? Was it my wife's spirit in the room?

I took the incident as being a sign from my wife. She was letting me know that she was okay—that she was watching over me, and that I was on the right path.

You may have lost someone you loved very much. While it is true that the physical body is no longer here, the spirit still is. Perhaps not as dramatically as I had experienced, but the spirit of the person you lost will always be with you. It will guide and encourage you.

Know that they are there for you whenever you need their support.

21 grams

I know you're there
Although it's nothing I can prove
I know you're there
From just the way the shadows move
And though I said goodbye and fin'ly let you go
I know you're there
Although I don't know how I know.
—Alix Korey, American composer

In 1907, researcher Duncan MacDougall found that 21 grams of body weight were lost immediately after a person died. He attributed the weight loss as a result of the soul leaving the body. The tests were never replicated and the results were widely dismissed by the scientific community. Still, it does bring up the question of what, if anything, remains when we die.

We may never be able to prove that the soul or spirit exists or whether it leaves the body upon death. But what we can be certain of is a lingering memory of those who have gone before us. And *that*, if nothing else, is the true soul or spirit of a living being.

It is that spirit of the deceased that we carry around with us in our thoughts. It is those memories that keep that person's essence alive. And, when we think or speak of that person, though the body may not be around anymore, that person's spirit continues forever.

larger than your loss

Adversity has the effect
of eliciting talents which,
in prosperous circumstances,
would have lain dormant.
                    —Horace, Roman Poet

When my wife died at the age of 34, I thought my life had ended.

How could I go on living without her?
How was I going to raise my young daughter alone?
What was I going to do with my life now?

What I didn't realize at the time, and what I couldn't possible know then, was that in the bigger picture, my wife's death was an important part of my life's intricate plan. She was here to lay the foundation for both me and my daughter and our own unique contributions to the betterment of the world, as well as to enrich our spiritual paths.

You are larger than your loss, which is why you will be able to survive it. And, paradoxically, your loss is larger than you, which is why it will teach you more than you ever imagined.

becoming bigger

Life is a series of experiences,
each of which makes us bigger,
even though it is hard to realize this.
For the world was built to develop character,
and we must learn that the setbacks and grieves
which we endure help us in our marching onward.
—Henry Ford, American industrialist

No matter how horrendous the loss you have experienced is, no matter how devastated you may be right now, you are bigger than your loss. You are stronger than your loss.

Right now, in the midst of your loss, you probably don't feel very strong. Someday, however, you may look back and see how this loss has given you the emotional and mental qualities you never realized you had.

51

Loss makes us larger. It helps us discover a force we had inside of us that perhaps we never knew we had. It gives us eyes to see new things and ears to listen to the world in new ways. It awakens our senses and helps us to realize the preciousness and incredible magnificence of life.

with a little help from your friends

*You think your pains and heartbreaks are
unprecedented in the history of the world,
but then you read. It was books that taught
me that the things that tormented me were
the very things that connected me with all the
people who were alive, or who have ever been alive.*
—James Baldwin, American author

Gypsies know that support is important in critical times. When a gypsy gets sick, a group of family members and friends accompany the person who is ill to the doctor.

Take a lesson from gypsies. Get help. Join a grief support group.

These groups were created to help you deal with your loss. Take advantage of them. They are there to support you. They will help you in your recovery process and help you realize that, in time, you will heal.

Being in a support group will also show you that you are not alone. You will see others who have gone through some of the same things you are going through. You will also see that they have successfully gotten through their loss.

And, with the shared tears and laughter of a group, you see that it is possible to live and even laugh again.

connect with others

A friend is the one who comes in
when the whole world has gone out.
—attributed to Grace Pulpit

In addition to a support group, you might also look for someone special who you know would bring the greatest comfort during your time of loss.

There were two of those people in my life when my wife died. One was a volunteer at a grief center and the other was my young daughter. The volunteer and I would meet once a week. She didn't offer advice on how I should overcome my grief. She simply told me her story of loss and I told her mine. We chatted; we laughed; we cried. We consoled and comforted each other.

The other person was my 10-year-old daughter. Yes, I

had the support of friends and family members, and yes, I even went to a therapist, but the biggest help was that of my young child. She was open, she was direct, and she gave me hope to go on when all else was seemingly lost.

Who is it that can sit with you, give you a hug, and be the shoulder you can cry on?

the power of hope

It's never the end of the world.
It's already tomorrow in Australia.
           –Charles M. Schulz, American cartoonist

During your loss, you may have been so angry or despondent that you blurted out a number of curse words, including some four-letter ones. But there is another four-letter word that might serve you better at this time. That word is "hope."

Hope is the greatest treasure you have.

When all else fails, hope is something to hang on to.

Don't give up.

the highest good

Higher Good is like water. It benefits us all.
                                    –The Tao Te Ching

When I grew up, we lived in a very Jewish neighborhood in the Bronx. If we went out to dinner, it would always be to the same Chinese restaurant. And we would order the same exact thing each week: one dish from column A and two dishes from column B.

In those days, from my limited perspective, I thought that everyone in the world was Jewish and that everyone ate at a Chinese restaurant on Sunday. It wasn't until I attended an out-of-town school and met people from all over the world that I realized that not everyone lived as I did.

Like my Bronx upbringing, our view of the universe is very limited. We cannot see beyond our lifespan. Thus, we cannot always see what is best for the universe as a whole.

The best we can do, therefore, is ask that what is happening to us — even if it be a major loss in our life — is for the highest good.

what's empty, fills

Nature abhors a vacuum.
—H. Emilie Cady, American physician/author

Sit quietly and try to empty your mind of any thoughts. For a few minutes, see if you cannot think of anything at all. You will probably find this very difficult to do, maybe near impossible. You might be able to do this for a few seconds or so, but chances are that as soon as one thought leaves, another rushes in to fill it.

Nature is like that too. Lift a rock in a river and water will immediately flow into the crevasse and fill it up again.

Like the void created by removing the rock in the river, something has been removed in your life and has created an empty space. Know that the emptiness is only temporary. Things cannot remain empty forever. When there is an empty space, it gets filled up again with something else.

That is a law of nature.

There is a space in your life right now. Take comfort in knowing that in time, it will be refilled. You may not yet know with what, or when, but it will.

opportunity knocks

After pain is always a new opportunity.
You can count on it, like the day following the night.
—Anthony Robbins, American self-help author/speaker

I grew up in New York City. So, I never really needed a car, owned one, or learned to drive. When my wife and I moved to San Francisco, she was the designated driver of the car we bought. When she died, the car sat in the driveway for six months. I would look at it every day and finally realized that I had to make a decision about it.

I could sell it. I could let it rust there. Or, I could learn to drive. I chose the latter.

Little did I realize at the time I learned to drive that I could never do the work I am currently doing — traveling around the country giving presentations on therapeutic humor — without having my driver's license. One part of my life ended with my loss, but another began.

Now that one part of your life has ended, another will begin.

Be patient.

seeds of the best

The worst thing in your life
may contain seeds of the best.
When you can see crisis as an opportunity
your life becomes not easier, but more satisfying.
                                        —Joe Kogel, American humorist

My wife's death allowed me to see things that I hadn't noticed before. It forced me to look inward to see my own finitude, my own beauty, and the beauty in others. Once I started to accept her death, my life opened up and became fuller and richer. Material things had less meaning for me, and my spiritual and inner growth became more important to me.

Perhaps, as the quotation above states, you can see your loss — "the worst thing in your life" — containing some seeds of the best. If you are having trouble doing that, consider the oyster. It takes an irritating piece of sand within its body and creates a glowing, radiant pearl.

What positive thing might come out of your loss?

Allen Klein

living and losing

Life does not accommodate you, it shatters you.
It is meant to and it couldn't do it better.
Every seed destroys its container
or else there would be no fruition.
—Florida Scott-Maxwell, American author

If you are alive, you will experience some loss in your life. That is the law of nature.

Think of a tree. In the fall, the leaves drop to the ground. In the winter, they decay and provide nourishment for the tree. In the spring, the tree blooms again—fuller, richer, and more radiant than before, because those fallen leaves fed it.

You are not much different than a tree.

The people you have lost are part of life's cycle. They live, they die, and they nurture those that come after them. You are one of those people. Be thankful that they have been in your life.

finding meaning in your loss

I know that they are in heaven ... and I know
that that's why this movement is growing because
we have tens of thousands of angels behind us that
are supporting us, that are saying, 'Well, you know
we died and that was really crappy, but we hope
that our deaths are going to make the world a better
place,' and it's up to us to make sure that it does.
—Cindy Sheehan, American anti-war activist

In his book *Man's Search for Meaning*, Viktor Frankl re-
lates a story about an elderly man who grieved for two years
over the death of his wife. Frankl asked the man, "What
would have happened ... if you had died first, and your wife
would have had to survive you?" The man answered, "Oh,
for her this would have been terrible; how she would have
suffered!" Frankl responded, "You see ... such a suffering

has been spared to her, and it was you who have spared her this suffering — to be sure, at the price that now you have to survive and mourn her."

Frankl observed, "In some way, suffering ceases to be suffering at the moment it finds a meaning."

What has happened to you has happened. You can't change that. But you can change what you do with it.

Can you find some meaning in your loss?

keeping your loved one alive

When we die, we die three times.
First, when our brain ceases to function.
Second, when our heart stops beating.
Third, when our name is no
longer spoken in the world.

—Jewish saying

My daughter was 10 years old when my wife died. The three years that we knew my wife had a terminal illness were a terrible strain on both of us. I realized after my wife's death that my daughter and I needed a reprieve from what we had been through; we needed an adventure. So I booked a trip to Alaska on the Inside Passage ferry system. And what an adventure it was. We went whitewater rafting, took seaplane rides, and spent the night next to a calving glacier.

Taking the trip was an instinctual decision but, looking back, a very wise one. It not only helped take our minds off of our loss, but it also helped us bond. That bonding allowed us to talk openly about Ellen's death. It made it easier to not hide our feelings or avoid conversations about our loss. It also allowed us to both laugh and cry together.

We would often talk about missing Ellen. Frequently, when we didn't quite know what to do in a situation, we would turn to each other and ask, "What would Mommy do?" And then do it her way. Often, we discussed Ellen as if she were alive and still part of our life, which, on some level, she was. And we continued to have those conversations, although less so as time went on.

To keep your loved one alive, learn from the lessons they have left for you and you will be speaking of them often.

wake-up call

*Most people don't know there are angels
whose only job is to make sure you don't get too
comfortable and fall asleep and miss your life.*
      –Brian Andreas, www.storypeople.com

In Thornton Wilder's play *Our Town*, a young woman named Emily dies and goes to heaven. On her first day there, she wants to return to earth for just one more day. She is granted her wish and is taken back in time. Home again, she notices that her family fails to appreciate the simple magnificence of life: the sunflowers, the food, the coffee, the new-ironed dresses, the hot baths, and sleeping and waking up. "Do any human beings," Emily poignantly asks, "ever realize life while they live it?"

Your loss may seem more like a curse now than a blessing, but someday you may understand why those you have lost were a Godsend. Those angels in disguise provided you with a wake-up call to appreciate the little things in life, for it is those little things that life is really all about.

closer to your core

*The most intense moments in our life,
like the losing someone very close to us,
can bring us closer to our core.
Because death is such a powerful force,
it awakens some fire in us and connects
to the deceased and the world around us.*
—Judy Tatelbaum, American author/therapist

After my wife died, I sold the silkscreen business I had. I knew that there was something else I was supposed to do in my life. I didn't know what that was, but silkscreening was not it. So I got rid of the business and hung out for a while, waiting to see what the universe would bring. Not long after, a catalog from the Holistic Life University came in the mail. One of the tracks they taught was about death and dying. I enrolled in the program, became the director of it several years later, and began my new journey.

I had no idea where any of this would take me, but I followed my gut. I gave up the business I owned, went down a new path, and followed my desire to teach people about the therapeutic value of humor. All this stemmed from a loss that brought me closer to my core and led me to my passion.

Be open to where your loss might lead you.

a new world

*When we are no longer able to
change a situation...we are
challenged to change ourselves.*
　　　　　　–Viktor Frankl, Austrian psychiatrist

Loss instantly changes your world. The once-familiar becomes strange. But, with time, the strange will become familiar.

The loss of someone you loved puts you in a whole new world — a world of living without them. It takes a lot of adjusting to get used to this new world and to move forward in it. Moving forward, however, does not imply forgetting those who are no longer with you. It just means that you will be leaving one chapter of your life behind you and moving on to the next one.

Like the chapters in a book, we know what was in the

preceding chapter, but we don't know what is to come. That's what makes books so interesting.

Not knowing what comes next can make life interesting too.

embrace change

Don't judge change as being either good or bad.
Just let it happen. One and the same thing can
at the same time be good, bad, and indifferent,
e.g., music is good to the melancholy, bad to those
who mourn, and neither good nor bad to the deaf.
—Baruch Spinoza, Dutch philosopher

While change may be unsettling, it is what every living thing is about. Everything changes, even the vast oceans of the world. Every day, their tides rise and fall dramatically.

I have learned a lot about change from a large ornamental plum tree out my kitchen window. It is constantly changing. In winter, it has no leaves. In spring, it has beautiful flowers. In summer, it has a small supply of plums. And in the fall, the leaves begin to drop as it starts its changing process all over again.

In her book *The First 30 Days*, author Ariane de Bonvoisin has a "Change Manifesto." Although she is writing about change in general, some of her suggestions are very relevant to dealing with change that occurs after a loss. Among them are:

Change is part of life and happens to everyone.

Change brings new people, new opportunities, and new perspectives.

Change helps me strengthen my...self-reliance, inner fortitude, and inner faith that I can handle anything.

Change is never punishment; it is always an opportunity to connect with what's inside of me.

Change reminds me that I am not in control of many things that happen and reminds me to let go and to surrender a little more to life.

Change helps me find my highest self—the part of me that is always there, that doesn't change. Life's unpredictability becomes infinitely easier when I connect with that part of myself.

Change is always on my side. It exists to serve me, teach me lessons, and help me embrace life's mysteries.

the human spirit

Man has never made any material
as resilient as the human spirit.
   –Bernard Williams, English philosopher

Your spirit may be down. Your spirit may feel like it is broken. That is only temporary.

Get up again.

Once you do, your spirit will begin to mend. Someday, your spirit will be whole again.

additional thoughts on learning

*We cannot live the afternoon of life
according to the program of life's morning,
for what was great in the morning will be
little at evening and what in the morning
was true, at evening will have become a lie.*
              —Carl Gustav Jung, Swiss psychiatrist

*Sometimes in the winds of change,
we find our direction.*

                                    —Anonymous

*When you have something like heart surgery,
you appreciate the simple things, like breathing.*
              —Robin Williams, American comedian

Step Three
letting go

The longer we dwell on our misfortunes,
the greater is their power to harm us.
                    —Voltaire, French philosopher

Crying is the body's way of dealing with loss. It is unhealthy to squelch your tears. What you stifle today may come back in greater force tomorrow. But continuing to endlessly wallow in those tears is not healthy. At some point, you need to get on with your life.

Today might be the day to take the first step, to let go, to move on.

things are different now

The pessimist complains about the wind;
the optimist expects it to change;
the realist adjusts the sails.
      −William Arthur Ward, American author

After your loss, things will be different. That doesn't mean they have to be bad.

How you view what has happened to you depends on whether you are a pessimist, an optimist, or a realist.

The wind has changed.

It may be time to adjust your sails.

bend without breaking

As I started to picture the trees in the storm, the answer began to dawn on me. The trees in the storm don't try to stand up straight and tall and erect. They allow themselves to bend and be blown with the wind. They understand the power of letting go. Those trees and those branches that try too hard to stand up strong and straight are the ones that break.
—Julia Butterfly Hill, American environmentalist

While writing this book, a friend, who was also a distant relative, passed away. It wasn't unexpected, since he had been under hospice care for the past few weeks. But it still hurt. It upset me even more because I already had airline tickets and was planning on visiting with him during my trip to New York City. But he had gone before I could get there. His death forced me to let go of my plans and expectations.

The incident made me realize how often in life we have to let go. For example, at home, our youngsters leave the house for the first time and go off to kindergarten or camp. Let go. Then they go off to college. Let go. Then they get married and permanently move away. Let go.

Then there is the world at work. You don't get the job or the raise you want. Let go. You are transferred to a new city. Let go. The boss you really like retires. Let go. Or, you retire and no longer have the job you had been doing for perhaps the past 30 to 40 years. Let go.

Then there is aging. You can't walk as far or as fast as you once did. Let go. You can't see or hear as well as you did previously. Let go.

And, finally, there is death — perhaps the ultimate letting go. Let go.

this too shall pass

The past cannot be changed.
The future is still in your power.
　　　　　　　　—Hugh White, American politician

Right now you may feel that there is nothing to live for. But remember, like everything else in life, nothing stays the same. Everything changes.

And this too shall pass.

change is inevitable

The only person who likes change is a wet baby.
—Roy Blitzer, management consultant

$\mathbf{M}$any years ago, I went to see the movie *Groundhog Day*. When the film was over, I took the elevator to the lobby of the theater complex. In the elevator, two young teenage boys were talking about the film. One said to the other, "I hated the movie. Nothing happens."

And if you know the film, the teenagers are right. Bill Murray's character finds himself repeating the same day over and over again. When he gets up each morning, the same song is playing on the radio, the same overnight blizzard has blanketed the area, and the same people are on the same street in the exact same place doing and saying the exact same thing they did the day before.

The movie is a great example of what would probably

happen if things never changed. Like the Murray character, you would be so totally bored that you would probably start to go nuts. Change is what makes life challenging and exciting.

Change happens. It is inevitable. And it is needed. Sometimes, we like it when things change. Sometimes, as in loss, we don't. But there is really not much we can do about it, except let go.

Allen Klein

losing and choosing

*Everything can be taken from a man but one thing:
the last of the human freedoms — to choose one's
attitude in any given set of circumstances,
to choose one's own way.*
—Viktor Frankl, Austrian psychiatrist/Holocaust survivor.

In one of my workshops, I asked a woman (a volunteer
director at a local hospital) what stressed her out the
most. She said that it was when volunteers don't show up.
I tried to give her some techniques to let go of this stress-
ful situation, but she refused to even consider these. The
more I suggested ways to lighten up the situation, the
more she held on to her upset, and, because of her continued stubbornness, the more the audience laughed.

Letting go is not easy, particularly after a loss. But, like
the woman above, you have a choice. You can let your grief

engulf your life or you can choose to begin to embrace life
again.

forgiving others

*One of the greatest struggles of the healing process
is to forgive both yourself and others and to stop
expending valuable energy on the past hurts.*
—Caroline Myss, American author

Before you can fully embrace life again, you need to let
go of any anger you have toward the person you lost. Carrying around that upset only gets in the way of truly experiencing life. That anger is like a stranglehold that person
still has on you even though that person may no longer be
around.

Forgive the deceased:

—for wanting more than you might have been capable
of giving

–for something they may have done or said that upset
  you
–for leaving you

And remember, just because your loved ones are no
longer around, you can still forgive them. It is not really
for them anyway; it is for you.

In addition to forgiving the deceased, you may also
want to forgive others who were involved in the loss too.

Forgive:

–the doctor who wasn't able to save your loved one
–a friend or relative who wasn't there for you
–anyone who can't sympathize with your loss

forgiving yourself

Forgiveness is a funny thing.
It warms the heart and cools the sting.
—William Arthur Ward, American author

If you want to let go and move on with your life, you need to not only forgive other people who may have hurt or disappointed you, but you also have to forgive yourself.

Forgive yourself:

- —for things you wanted to say to the deceased but did not
- —for not being able to bring back your loved one
- —for any guilt you are having now that they are gone

Healing begins to happen when you can forgive yourself.

keep on forgiving

Forgiveness does not change the past,
but it does enlarge the future.
                    —Paul Boese, Dutch botanist

When dealing with a loss, people try to be helpful. Sometimes, however, they say the wrong thing and are more hurtful than helpful.

If someone makes you angry by saying things like, "It's probably for the best," "Don't take it so hard," or "Life is difficult," realize that people sometimes have a hard time being around death and dying situations. They mean well but don't always know the most comforting thing to say or do.

Forgive them too.

ask others for forgiveness

*He that cannot forgive others breaks the
bridge over which he must pass himself;
for everyman has need to be forgiven.*
  —Edward Herbert, British diplomat

Just as we must forgive ourselves and others, in order to
move on, it is important to ask for forgiveness from others.

Dealing with a loss can be all consuming. While you
were in the midst of that turmoil, were you:

—curt with someone who was trying to help?
—forgetting to thank people for their support?
—not communicating well with friends and family?

Ask them to forgive you.

Do you also need to ask forgiveness from the deceased:

–for not doing more to help them?
–for not being as compassionate as
  they wanted you to be?
–for not being able to save them?

Ask them to forgive you too.

inner peace

Take a leap in faith and trust in love, trust God.
Choose to experience peace rather than conflict.
Choose to experience love rather than fear and guilt.
Choose to be a love finder rather than a faultfinder.
Choose to be a love—giver rather than a love-seeker.
Teach only love for that is what you are.
    —Gerald Jampolsky, American psychiatrist

Once you have forgiven other people as well as the person you have lost, and yourself, you will begin to experience inner peace. It is from that place that you can now let go and allow the joy of life to once again enter your world.

look within

I shut my eyes in order to see.
—Paul Gauguin, French artist

Sometimes, when someone dies, there is so much commotion among family members and friends that it is hard to think clearly. Those people mean well, but you may need a little time for yourself.

Sit quietly for a while with your thoughts and your feelings.

In a somewhat playful manner, Martin Boroson, author of *One-Moment Meditation*, suggests a very simple, very short way to look inside in order to, as he calls it, "refresh your browser."

Close your eyes and shift your focus from what you were looking at to what you can hear.

As you listen to the sounds around you, without judging them or even identifying them, breathe deeply.

Then open your eyes and shift your focus back to what you can see...now with fresh eyes.

You have refreshed your browser.

remember to breathe

*Breathe. Let go. And remind yourself
that this very moment is the only
one you know you have for sure.*
      −Oprah Winfrey, American television host

It may sound silly to remind you to breathe, since breathing is such a natural state. But when you are under stress, your breaths become shallow. You tighten up and forget just how calming slow, deep breathing can be.

Some simple, breathing-related phrases might remind you to keep taking slow, deep breaths:

      −to get ones breath back
      −to breathe freely again
      −to breathe confidently
      −to breathe new life into something

–to breathe a sigh of relief

Now, take a slow, deep breath and let go.

let go of the past

*You can clutch the past so tightly
to your chest that it leaves your arms
too full to embrace the present.*
        —Jan Glidewell, American columnist

What has happened in the past has happened. There is absolutely nothing you can do to bring your loved one back.

But you can let go of the past, live in the present, and be hopeful about the future.

rejoice in a life lived

*When a child is born, all rejoice; when someone
dies, all weep. But it makes just as much sense,
if not more, to rejoice at the end of a life as at
the beginning. For no one can tell what events
await a newborn child, but when a mortal
dies he has successfully completed a journey.*
                                                    —The Talmud

Right now you may be mourning for a life lost. But you
can also celebrate that life lived.

Celebrate the good times you had together.

Celebrate how the deceased enriched your world.

Celebrate the wonderful things that person meant to
you.

And remember, it doesn't matter how long that loved
one's life was. Like a beautiful symphony, it is the beauty
of the music that matters — not the length of the piece.

trust your gut

Follow your instincts.
That's where true wisdom manifests itself.
—Oprah Winfrey, American television host

"When a train goes through a tunnel and it gets dark," wrote Holocaust survivor Corrie ten Boom, "you don't throw away the ticket and jump off. You sit still and trust the engineer."

You may feel that you are in a dark tunnel right now. But tunnels don't go on forever. At some point, they end. As the old cliché says, there is always light at the end of the tunnel.

At some point in your despair, you will realize that you cannot stay in this dark place forever. Something inside of you will tell you that it is time to move on.

Listen to that inner voice.

additional thoughts on letting go

*Hanging onto resentment is letting someone
you despise live rent-free in your head.*
  −Ann Landers, American syndicated columnist

*Whatever you think people are withholding
from you—give it to them.... Soon after you
start giving, you will start receiving.*
  −Eckhart Tolle, German spiritual teacher

*When I let go of what I am,
I become what I might be.*
  −Lao Tzu, Chinese philosopher

Step Four
living

I can choose to sit in perpetual sadness,
immobilized by the gravity of my loss,
or I can choose to rise from the pain
and treasure the most precious
gift I have — life itself.
–Walter Anderson, American magazine editor

The loss of someone close to you provides an opportunity for a new beginning and an enriched life. Once you start to work through your grief process, you can begin to fill the vacuum that was created by your loss with an even fuller sense of life.

Ultimately, in dealing with a loss, the choice is yours. No matter what the situation, you have a choice of how you react to it. You can remain in your grief and turn your face away from life or you can move on and embrace life.

Choose life.

getting on with life

Being fully alive to life is truly a heroic act.
Many of us think heroism means rescuing people
from burning buildings or being daring in wartime.
Instead, heroism is an everyday affair. For some
of us, getting up in the morning and facing another
day is a heroic act. For others, changing jobs, losing
jobs, or living with health problems, or staying in a
relationship or managing on limited funds or facing
the loss of a loved one is a heroic act. We have many
opportunities to be heroes in our daily lives. The
heroism of which I speak is the courage to be fully
alive to life, regardless of our circumstances.
—Judy Tatelbaum, American author/therapist

Sometimes after a loss, it feels like you too are in the land of the dead. At some point, you need to move to the land of the living and get on with your life.

Sitting around bemoaning your loss only gets you deeper into a downward spiral. At some point, no matter how hard it might be, if you are to heal from your loss, you must do something other than wallow in it. You must start living again.

If you don't, you will have created a double loss — the person who has died and the loss of your own spirit.

to live again

*The person who removes a mountain
begins by carrying away small stones.*
                              —Chinese proverb

Sometimes the first step is the hardest.

But, remember, without that first step, there is no second.

To fully live life again, take the first step.

take back your life

*When we hate our enemies, we are giving
them power over us: power over our sleep,
our appetites, our blood pressure, our health
and our happiness. Our enemies would dance
with joy if only they knew how they were worrying
us, lacerating us, and getting even with us! Our
hate is not hurting them at all, but our hate is
turning our days and nights into a hellish turmoil.*
—Dale Carnegie, American writer

You may feel that your life has been robbed. Something
very precious has been taken away from you. That may be
true. Yet one simple uplifting thought can change that feeling.

A letter I received from a woman who found an inspiring quotation in one of my books showed me how the power of just a few words can help overcome a terrible incident. The woman wrote:

"At the age of 12, I was violently raped twice. I have never told anyone, but it haunted me for 55 years. It affected me in every aspect of my life. I was constantly filled with anger and rage. In reading your book, one phrase stood out — 'When we hate our enemies, we give them power over us. Our sleep, our health….' Because of that quotation, I have taken my power back and it has changed my life."

Can you find a quotation, a phrase, a song, a prayer, or a poem that will help you take back your life?

it takes effort

*To think bad thoughts is really the easiest thing
in the world. If you leave your mind to itself it
will spiral down into ever increasing unhappiness.
To think good thoughts, however, requires effort.*
—James Clavell, British/American novelist

Some days it may take all the effort you have to get out of bed.

Make the effort.

Some days it takes effort just to smile.

Smile anyway.

Some days it may be difficult to find one thing to be

happy about.

Keep seeking.

Pulling yourself out of your loss may take effort. But it is worth it. You are worth it. Make the effort.

keep moving

Life leaps like a geyser for those
who drill through the rock of inertia.
                    —Alexis Carrel, French physician

A friend and colleague of mine, Carl Hammerschlag, told me a wonderful story about the key to living life fully:

"I was in New York's Metropolitan Museum of Art when an old woman comes up to me and says, 'Excuse me, young man. Can you tell me what time it is?' I look at my watch and say, 'It's exactly two o'clock.' She tells me that she had a two o'clock appointment with friends, but they aren't here. Then, she continues on, without a comma or period, that she was rarely late for appointments, knew nothing about primitive art, worked at the Bronx Botanical Gardens. I'm daydreaming, looking at her, five-foot-two-inches, neatly dressed in a blue suit with a matching pillbox hat. In her white-gloved hand, she is carrying a handbag. Politely trying to get away, I hear her say, 'That's the secret of life.' I know I've missed something so I ask her, 'What's the secret of life?' And she says, 'Sneakers are the secret of life.' I have no idea what she is talking about, but as I look down more carefully, I see that accompanying her Easter ensemble, she is wearing sneakers. I know I've missed something so I ask her, 'How are sneakers the secret of life?' And she repeats, 'I wear these sneakers because they are only comfortable when you keep moving. That's the secret of life; you gotta keep moving.'

So now that you know the secret of life, put on your sneakers and keep moving.

get out of the house

A ship is safe in harbor,
but that's not what ships are for.
—William Shedd, American Presbyterian theologian

While cleaning out my closet, I found a jar that contained some seashells I had found on a beach many years ago. They had attractive shapes and colors, but I remember how much more brilliant they were when I first found them on the beach. In the jar, they were still pretty, but they lost their luster; they didn't have the glow they once had.

When you are dealing with a loss, becoming a hermit in your residence may seem like an easy way out. You don't have to deal with an unsympathetic world. It feels comfortable. It is safe.

However, staying at home — particularly if you lived in

the same household with the deceased — you are constantly surrounded by memories of that person. It will only bring you down. If you wait for your grief to completely go away, which it rarely does, you will never do anything.

Get out of the house. Have lunch with friends. Go to a movie or a museum. Nothing happens when you stay at home.

Like those shells in the jar, you need to get away from your container in order to regain your luster and lust for life.

As scary as it seems, you must get out of the house.

do it anyway

*Life is risky; we are all acrobats
tiptoeing over one bridge or another.
To a tightrope walker the rope is just
like home. Those who hold their bodies
lightly and their minds simply may
seem in danger, but they are safe.*
—Chinese scroll saying

Recently I received an email from a woman who lost her young husband in a car crash. She said that with his death, her "life has not and never will be the same."

And she is right. It never will be the same. But that does not mean that her life, or yours after your loss, cannot be fulfilling.

One of the things that death teaches us is that life is short; if you want to do something, you probably should not put it off or you may never get to do it. Death also teaches us that life is filled with risks and that we need to take some of those risks if we are to reap life's rewards.

After my wife died, I realized it was time to confront some of those risks and do things I had been putting off for years. I learned to drive a car for the first time at the age of 42. I went back to school again to get my master's degree. I gave up a business I co-owned and started a new one.

In spite of your loss and the feeling that your life may never be the same, the death of a loved one can bring a surprisingly new life. I encourage you to seek yours.

What small risk can you take today that might help you live fully again?

do something new

*I have always been delighted
at the prospect of a new day, a
fresh try, one more start, with
perhaps a bit of magic waiting
somewhere behind the morning.*
—J. B. Priestly, English author

One of the things that can happen when you are dealing with a loss is that you also lose your incentive to try new things. It is safer to stay where you are — to remain in your comfort zone.

To begin to live fully again, you need to step out of your comfort zone. Start small. Tomorrow, get out of your rut by:

—wearing something bright

—dining at a restaurant you've seen but never tried
—taking a walk or a drive to somewhere you have
  never been before

life is short
Carpe Diem (Seize the Day)
—Horace, Roman poet

On December 8, 2009, there was an article in USA Today that read:

A worker was killed when a slab of granite fell on him inside a construction supply store Monday. Police said the man, 47, was working in the store when granite fell on his head. The victim's name was withheld pending notification of his family.

We never know when, or how, death will come. We don't know when we wake up in the morning if we will still be around that evening. While this not-knowing may be unsettling, it can also be enlivening. It teaches us that, no matter how long we have on this earth, life is finite and we need to live fully each day.

Losing someone you love awakens you to the fact that

you too have limited time on earth. What are you going to do with the time you have left? Are you going to continually mourn your loss or get on with your life?

life is a gift

*Reflect upon your present blessings, of
which every man has many — not on your past
misfortunes, of which all men have some.*
                    —Charles Dickens, English novelist

Look around. What do you have right now?

Sure, you have lost something you love, but you haven't lost everything. If nothing else, if you are still breathing, you have the gift of life.

Perhaps it is time to open that gift and enjoy it.

help yourself by helping others

When a man is singing and cannot lift his voice,
and another comes and sings with him,
another who can lift his voice,
the first will be able to lift his voice too.
That is the secret of the bond between spirits.
—Hasidic saying

Author Leo Buscaglia was once asked to judge a contest to discover the most caring child. The winner was a four-year-old whose next-door neighbor—an elderly gentleman—had recently lost his wife. Upon seeing the man cry, the little boy climbed onto the old gentleman's lap and sat there silently. When his Mother asked what he had said to the neighbor, the little boy replied, "Nothing; I just helped him cry."

Perhaps the biggest comfort you can give another human being who is experiencing a loss is to simply be with them. If laughter comes up when you are with them, laugh. If tears arise when you are with them, cry.

Spending time with someone who has been through a similar situation to yours can show you that you too can be a survivor. As you begin to emerge from your loss, it may be time to help others with theirs.

god helps those who help themselves

Remember, if you ever need a helping hand,
you'll find one at the end of your arm .... As
you grow older you will discover that you
have two hands. One for helping yourself,
the other for helping others.
—Audrey Hepburn, British actress

Reaching out and helping others is a wonderful way to put your loss in the background. It helps lift you up while doing the same for other people. But you also need to help yourself and make time to nurture and nourish the most important person in your life right now...you.

Get a massage.

Soak in the tub.

Go see an uplifting movie.

Send yourself a greeting card.

Take an afternoon nap.

allow others to do something for you

None of us has gotten where we are
solely by pulling ourselves up from
our own bootstraps. We got here
because somebody bent down and helped us.
–Thurgood Marshall, U.S. Supreme Court judge

Sometimes we think that it is better to give than receive. While that may be true sometimes, now, in your time of need, it is your turn to receive.

Others may want to do things for you.
Allow them to do it.

You may feel that you don't deserve it.
You do.

Allen Klein

You may feel that you can do it yourself.
You can, but let other people help anyway.

Allow other people to:

    –cook you a meal
    –drive you to an appointment
    –take you to an event
    –spend time with you
    –comfort you

be thankful

*He is a man of sense who does
not grieve for what he has not,
but rejoices in what he has.*
                    −Epictetus, Greek philosopher

One of my spiritual teachers would often remind me that, "To want what you don't have, is to waste what you do have."

When you are going through a loss it may feel like everything is lost. It is not. You still have a lot in your life to be thankful for.

Instead of focusing on what you don't have anymore, be grateful for what you do have. Tomorrow morning, before you get out of bed, think of at least one thing that you are thankful for. And then, when you get out of bed, start writing down all the wonderful things in your life. You can be thankful for:

    –a penny you find on the street
    –the cookies a neighbor brought you
    –the friends you have
    –a rainbow
    –a compliment
    –flowers in the park
    –a cup of tea

simple pleasures

I have never been a millionaire,
but I have enjoyed a great meal,
a crackling fire, a glorious sunset,
a walk with a friend, a hug from a
child, a cup of soup, a kiss behind
the ear. There are plenty of
life's tiny delights for all of us.
—attributed to Jack Anthony

One action you can take to put your loss in the background for a while is to focus on the little things you like — the little things that bring you joy.

What are the simple little things that bring you pleasure?

—A double latte?

–A certain TV show?
–A visit to your garden?
–Listening to your favorite music?
–The sound of birds chirping?

half full or half empty?

*Some people are always grumbling
because roses have thorns.
I am thankful that thorns have roses.*
— Alphonse Karr, French journalist

You may or may not believe in the power of positive thinking. But even if you don't, what harm would it do to try?

Positive thinking is not about lying to yourself; it is about recognizing what is good about a situation in spite of what you don't like about it.

Tomorrow, catch yourself every time you have a negative thought. Then see if you can find a positive one to replace it.

shine your light

You cannot cause a shadow to disappear
by trying to fight it, stomp on it, by railing
against it, or any other form of emotional
or physical resistance. In order to cause a
shadow to disappear, you must shine light on it.
—Shakti Gawain, American teacher/author

The loss you have experienced may have dimmed your enthusiasm for life. But your light hasn't gone out. It just isn't as bright now as it used to be.

Find something to nurture that light.
Find something you love to do.
Find something you can do to help a hurting world.

And you will burn bright again.
Perhaps even brighter than before.

a chance to rise higher

*Live your life each day as you would climb
a mountain. An occasional glance toward
the summit keeps the goal in mind, but many
beautiful scenes are to be observed from each
new vantage point. Climb slowly, steadily,
enjoying each passing moment; and the
view from the summit will serve as
a fitting climax for the journey.*
        –attributed to Harold B. Melchart

You may feel down in the dumps. You may feel that you
will never rise up from that place. Yet, every day is a chance
to move upward.

What can you do today to take one more step on the
healing ladder, to take one more step toward fully embracing life again?

139

moving on

*When your car tank is empty, you don't sit
and get depressed and think it's permanent.
You go fill it up. It's the same with life—when
you're running on empty, go fill up your
tank with a better thought, emotion
or action and get on with life.*
   —Esther Hicks, American author/speaker

Loss often makes you feel like you are stuck. It is paralyzing. You feel a heaviness weighing you down. You have trouble moving. You feel you can't possibly go on.

But you can.

If you are reading this book, you are probably ready to move on. Your loss may feel overwhelming, but now that you have come this far, you can go further.

Your loss may have thrown you off track for a while, but the tracks are still there. All you need to do is get back on them.

yesterday

Don't let yesterday use up too much of today.
　　　　　　　—Will Rogers, American humorist

I once heard it said that you can vote on yesterday but you can't veto it.

What has happened has happened. You can't change that. It is already done.

But you can decide how you will mark your ballot and choose how you will handle things from now on.

today

*Nobody can go back and
start a new beginning,
but anyone can start today
and make a new ending.*
—attributed to Maria Robinson

Today is really all we have.

Yesterday is a memory. Tomorrow is a fantasy.

No matter how you are feeling today, celebrate it. Today will be gone tomorrow and too late to enjoy.

Live your life today before it becomes yesterday.

tomorrow

Courage does not always roar.
Sometimes, it is the quiet voice at the end
of the day saying, "I will try again tomorrow."
—Mary Anne Radanbacher, American artist/writer

Although your loss may feel overwhelming today, tomorrow may be different.

There are a number of clichés about the hope that tomorrow can bring, such as:

"The sun will come out tomorrow."
"Tomorrow is another day."
"After the rain comes a rainbow."

Clichés may seem overused and predictable, but still, they are clichés because they have a ring of truth about them. No matter how cloudy today might seem to you, the sun will indeed come out tomorrow—or at least, the day after, or the one after that. It never stays cloudy forever.

The wonderful thing about life is that each day presents us with a new opportunity to leave yesterday behind.

time heals

Time heals all wounds,
unless you pick at them.
　　　－Shawn Alexander, American athlete

Another often-heard cliché related to loss is that "time heals everything."

I am not sure that is totally true. Time helps us heal but perhaps not everything. And perhaps it is not time that is the healer but what we do with that time.

What are you going to do today to help heal?

look around

*Every day we wake up, we are offered the world's
greatest buffet. It spreads as far as the eye can
see with vats of pleasure and joy, laughter and
smiles, happiness and contentment. It is available
to all. It is bought and paid for. Yet we take only
a tiny salad plate to this fabulous spread
and serve ourselves a few mere morsels.*
—Susan Sparks, American spiritual teacher

Several years ago, as an experiment, the world-renowned violinist Joshua Bell played at the entrance to one of the world's busiest subway stations. What the researchers discovered was the sad fact that few people took the opportunity to stop and hear this incredible free concert. Most rushed by ignoring a rare, once-in-a-lifetime opportunity to hear Bell play on a violin worth 3.5 million dollars.

Allen Klein

There is such an abundance of joyful things in this world, yet most of us don't stop and hear the music — or smell the roses — even when it is right in front of us.

Stop for a few moments today and look around you.

What have you missed seeing in your environment that can bring you more joy and help you to live more fully?

bitter-sweetness of life

*A man traveling across a field encountered a tiger.
He fled, the tiger after him. Coming to a precipice,
he caught hold of the root of a wild vine and swung
himself down over the edge. The tiger sniffed at him
from above. Trembling, the man looked down to
where, far below, another tiger was waiting to eat
him. Only the vine sustained him. Meanwhile, two
mice started to gnaw away the vine. The man saw
a luscious strawberry near him. Grasping the
vine with one hand, he plucked the strawberry
with the other. How sweet it tasted!*

–The Buddha

In the midst of loss, life may seem unsettling and bitter.
That, at times, may be true. But life, at times, is also sweet.
The bittersweet quality of life is ever present.

149

Like Buddha's parable above, we can have danger and the presence of death nearby, yet still find sweetness in life.

Can you reach out today to pluck a strawberry and find some sweetness among the sadness?

Learning to Laugh When You Feel Like Crying

life goes on

*I have found that life persists in the midst
of destruction and, therefore, there must
be a higher law than that of destruction.*
  —Mahatma Gandhi, Indian spiritual leader

In the play *The Skin of Our Teeth*, playwright Thornton Wilder writes about the Antrobus family who suffer incredible devastation as they combat all the horrors that befell man throughout the ages. They battle dinosaurs, they deal with ice age flooding, and they confront famine and plagues. In each case, they survive by "the skin of their teeth."

In spite of all the hardships the family endures, one of the characters strongly advises us "not to inquire why or whither, but just enjoy your ice cream while it's on your plate."

Can you take that advice to heart today and enjoy your ice cream before it melts?

additional thoughts on living

*It's only when we truly know and understand
that we have a limited time on earth—and that
we have no way of knowing when our time is
up—that we will begin to live each day to the
fullest, as if it was the only one we had.*
—Elisabeth Kübler-Ross, Swiss-born psychiatrist

*When someone we love dies,
we get so busy mourning what
died that we ignore what didn't.*
—Ram Dass, spiritual teacher

*I like living. I have sometimes been wildly,
despairingly, acutely miserable, racked with
sorrow, but through it all I still know quite
certainly that just to be alive is a grand thing.*
—Agatha Christie, British writer

153

Step Five
laughing

Tragedy and comedy are but two aspects
of what is real, and whether we see the tragic
or the humorous is a matter of perspective.
–Arnold Beisser, American polio-disabled author

It may seem ludicrous putting laughter and loss in the same sentence. How can you possibly laugh after losing a loved one? Yet recent research by Dacher Keltner and George A. Bonanno shows that "the more widows and widowers laughed and smiled during the early months after their spouse's death, the better their mental health was over the first two years of bereavement."

Laughter is a great coping mechanism. Finding the humor in anything and laughing about it gives you a break from the pain of loss. It allows for a breath of fresh air at a time when everything seems dark and heavy.

Many of the world's top comedians intuitively knew this when they experienced a major loss in their life. They turned to humor to cope and eventually perfected their craft and made comedy their career.

Your goal is probably not to become a stand-up comic, but you can take a lesson from these renowned comedians and use humor and laughter to help you to cope with your loss.

Laughter and humor are one of God's gifts to overcome your trials and tribulations.

laughter and tears

And the self-same well from which your laughter
rises was often-times filled with your tears.
        −Kahlil Gibran, Lebanese/American poet

It is okay to cry. Tears wash away harmful toxins in your body that build up when you are stressed and grieving. They help cleanse and wash away your sorrow.

But tears can also stop you from embracing and enjoying life. At some point, you need to curtail your crying in order to get on with your life.

When you stop crying, it doesn't mean that you loved the person you lost any less, or that you have forgotten them. It only means that you are ready to put your loss in the background for a while and let life unfold again.

And that involves learning to live and, yes, even laugh again.

appropriate, timely, and tasteful

*If humor is something like a sword, maybe it has
to be strapped on, but nobody should go around
without it in any period of time .... Since one of
its chief constituents is taste, it should be used
sparingly sometimes and left in its sheath at
other times, but it should always be handy.*
        —James Thurber, American author

A long time ago, a friend of mine was having a difficult
time dealing with the breakup of a long-term relationship.
He was explaining what had happened between him and
his partner. I tried cheering him up and offered a light-
hearted remark or two, which, I learned later, offended
him. He didn't think I took his "serious situation" serious
enough.

When you feel like crying, you often don't feel like

laughing. In fact, when you are in those down times, anything funny may seem offensive.

While laughter can be beneficial during and after a loss, you may not be ready for it. Don't force it. Just know that even though your lighter side is in hiding right now, it is still there and may appear when you least expect it.

how can you laugh at a time like this?

I think laughter may be a form of courage.
As humans we sometimes stand tall and look
into the sun and laugh, and I think we are
never more brave than when we do that.
                    —Linda Ellerbee, American journalist

Many people feel guilty when they laugh during a loss. They ask, "How can you laugh at a time like this?" Since laughter can be as healing as tears, the question, perhaps, should really be, "How can you not laugh at a time like this?"

If something funny happens, laugh. If something funny doesn't happen, don't laugh. Just don't ignore the laughter when something strikes your funny bone.

Sometimes, people feel guilty laughing when someone has died or they are dealing with a life-challenging situation. As long as you are not laughing at the deceased, the grieving, or the ill person, laughter can be as healing as tears.

Allow for both the tears and the laughter.

don't compare

*Laughter has always brought me out of
unhappy situations. Even in your darkest
moment, you usually can find something
to laugh about if you try hard enough.*
         —Red Skelton, American comedian

Every person's funny bone is in a different place. I love
Woody Allen. I even find something I like and something
to laugh about in his not-so-great movies. Other people
like the put-down humor of Don Rickles, or the absurd
humor of stand-up comedian Steve Wright, or the family-
friendly humor of Bill Cosby.

Who, or what, makes you laugh? Get more of those
people, or things, in your life.

humor buddies

Let us be grateful to people who make
us happy; they are the charming
gardeners who make our souls blossom.
— Marcel Proust, French novelist

I laugh a lot with some people. I hardly laugh at all with others.

Find those people — friends, acquaintances, cartoonists, comedians, or entertainers — who bring a smile to your face.

If they are friends, colleagues, or acquaintances, call them now.

If they are professional comedians or comic actors, watch one of their movies or TV shows.

If they are cartoonists, keep their cartoons where you can see them often.

give it time

Comedy is a tragedy plus time.
     –Carol Burnett, American comedian

As noted earlier, it has been said that time heals everything.

That doesn't mean that you will ever forget your loved one. What it means is that in time, your loss will not seem as enormous as it does now.

What it also means is that at some point, it will be possible to laugh again.

open to laughter

*Lightness of touch and living in the
moment are intertwined. One cannot dance
well unless one is completely in time with the
music, not leaning back to the last step or
pressing forward to the next one, but poised
directly on the present step as it comes.*
–Anne Morrow Lindbergh, American aviator/author

There is always something to laugh about. The problem
is that when we are stressed out, or in the grieving process, we may not see it. But it is still there. Something funny
might be right next to us but, like a horse with blinders,
we don't see or hear it because we are only focusing on our
loss.

Take off those blinders. Be open to laughter. And don't
squelch it when it comes because, as comedian Fred Allen

reminds us, "It is bad to suppress laughter. It goes back down and spreads to your hips."

laughter and loss

Life does not cease to be funny when
people die any more than it ceases
to be serious when people laugh.
　　　　　　—George Bernard Shaw, Irish dramatist

Serious illness, death, dying, and tragedies are no laughing matter. Things happen that aren't funny. Still, funny things happen.

If you think they don't, consider:

—the hospital gown ("Now I know why they call it I.C.U.")
—an open casket where someone says, "She never looked so good."
—a tombstone that reads, "See, I told you I was sick."

to laugh again

*Be of good cheer. Do not think of today's failures,
but of the success that may come tomorrow. You
have set yourselves a difficult task, but you will
succeed if you persevere; and you will find
a joy in overcoming obstacles.*
—Helen Keller, American blind/deaf author

Because of the intense loss you are experiencing, you may feel that you have also lost your sense of humor. You haven't lost it. It is just misplaced. You can, and will, find it again.

Keep looking.

Today, tell yourself that you will find one little thing of hope, one little thing that amuses you, one little thing to smile or laugh about.

If you can do that, you have taken a big step in your healing process.

let it begin with you

Beginning with the early dawn each day,
I will radiate joy to everyone I meet. I will
be mental sunshine for all who cross my path.
I will burn candles of smiles in the bosoms
of the joyless. Before the unfading light
of my cheer, darkness will take flight.
–Paramahansa Yogananda, Indian mediation teacher

If you are to find any joy in your life after your loss, it must begin with you. Others can guide you and show you the way, but they cannot do it for you. You need to find that joy inside of yourself.

Perhaps you can begin with a smile.

start with a smile

*Sometimes your joy is the source
of your smile, but sometimes your
smile can be the source of your joy.*
      —Thich Nhat Hanh, Buddhist monk

After a loss, it may take time to regain your laughter. That is understandable. It may even be difficult to smile. But that is a good place to start since research has shown that smiling produces effects conducive to healing. Smiling creates a cooler blood, resulting in sensations of calm and happiness. Frowning, on the other hand, creates warmer blood, resulting in feelings of sadness and anger.

So, smile when you wake up because the sun is shinning.

Smile when you wake up because it is raining.

Smile because you wake up.

healing humor

Always laugh when you can.
It is cheap medicine.
—Lord Byron, English poet

Healing doesn't mean that you are cured. It means that you are moving towards getting better. The Old English definition of healing means "to restore to sound health." And that is what a little laughter can do.

The crying times may still come, but a little laughter from time to time can help you get some distance from your loss and help heal your wounds.

tension release

*Laughter lets me relax. It's the
equivalent of taking a deep breath,
letting it out and saying, "This too will pass."*
                              —Odette Pollar, American author

When someone is dying, feelings are often raw, conversations stilted, and emotions run high. One of the important benefits of finding something funny, even in a crisis, is that laughter eases tensions and brings people together.

For example, one hospice nurse arrived at a family's home just after they put the patient on a bedside commode. While the nurse and the family were in the room, the patient had a bowel movement that was accompanied by a lot of loud noises. At first, everyone pretended that they heard nothing. Then, a young grandchild, overwhelmed by the smell, yelled out, "Geeesh, Grandma!" and quickly ran out

173

of the room. Everyone erupted in laughter. The incident broke the tension and created a bonding among the family. From then on, the nurse observed, the family shared easily.

humor and survival

*If you can find humor in
anything ... you can survive it.*
−Bill Cosby, American comedian

We don't often think of humor and laughter as a survival mechanism. We forget that when we "laugh it off," we are actually doing just that.

If you can laugh, even just a little, it shows you that there is light at the end of the tunnel.

A little bit of laughter shows you that you can go on ...

that you will survive.

the power of humor

*A sense of humor ... is needed armor. Joy
in one's heart and some laughter on one's
lips is a sign that the person down deep
has a pretty good grasp on life.*
                              —Hugh Sidey, American journalist

When you can find something to laugh about during
your grieving process, you have taken a step toward free-
ing yourself from that loss.

Laughter frees us. When we laugh, we are no longer
engulfed in our sorrow. We have broken free and affirmed
that we can rise above our circumstance. The smallest
amount of laughter can show you that you are not permanently stuck in a downward spiral. You can, even if only
momentarily, start that climb up again.

No one has the power to stop death. But we all have the

power to laugh in the face of it and not let death take away our joy of living.

As one author noted, "With laughter, death is less of a grave matter."

the power to rise above

Humor is an affirmation of dignity,
a declaration of man's superiority
to all that befalls him.
—Romain Gary, French writer

Viktor Frankl used humor to give him hope during his incarceration in a German concentration camp.

Captain Gerald Coffee used humor to deal with his seven-year confinement as a prisoner of war in North Vietnam.

Kathy Buckley, Alex Valdez, and Brett Leake are, respectively, deaf, blind, and a person with muscular dystrophy. All of them rise above what life has handed them by using humor in their stand-up comedy acts.

If they can find something to laugh about in their challenging situations, you can too.

softening the blow

*For me, if you are able to laugh,
you are the owner of the world.*
— Roberto Benigni, Italian actor

You have been hit with a loss. Humor and laughter will never change that. But they can soften the blow.

A good laugh can:

—divert your thinking away from your troubles
—balance your sadness
—connect you to other people
—help you calm down
—make you feel that life is worth living

Dealing with a major loss is draining. You may feel like you are running on empty. Finding something to laugh about, even for just a few seconds, can help to fill you up again.

Laughter is the juice of life. Squeeze all the energy you can out of it.

finding happiness again

*The way to happiness: keep your heart free
from hate, your mind from worry. Live simply,
expect little, give much. Fill your life with love.
Scatter sunshine. Forget self, think of others.
Do as you would be done by. Try this for
a week and you will be surprised.*
—Norman Vincent Peale, minister/author

During your loss, it may seem that you will never be happy again. It may seem that way right now, but that is only now.

Looking back in 10 days, 10 weeks, 10 months, or 10 years, you will probably feel differently about your loss than you do today.

Can you even imagine what your life will be like in those future days, weeks, months, or years? It may be difficult for you to see yourself as being happy during that time. But happiness is available. Wait. You'll see.

uplifting words

Loving words cost but little
Journeying up the hill of life;
But they make the weak and weary
Stronger, braver, for the strife.
Do you count them only trifles
What to earth are sun and rain?
Never was a kind word wasted;
Never was one said in vain.

—Anonymous

Words are powerful. They can lift you up. They can bring you down. What you are reading now has the power to heal and change your thinking. Similarly, the words you constantly say to yourself are equally as powerful to heal.

Watch what you say today and notice if your words are helping you overcome your loss or bringing you further down into it.

Look for words that lift your spirit, that make your heart sing, and fill you with joy. Words such as:

–Amusing
–Cheery
–Delightful
–Enjoyable
–Happy
–Hopeful
–Jolly
–Joyful
–Laughing
–Merry
–Pleasing
–Pleasurable
–Smiling
–Wonderful

positive self-talk

Watch your thoughts, for they become words.
Watch your words, for they become actions.
Watch your actions, for they become habits.
Watch your habits, for they become character.
Watch your character, for it becomes your destiny.

—Anonymous

What you tell yourself about your loss is a good indicator of how you will recover from it. Are you telling yourself, "I will pull through this somehow," or are you saying, "I will never get over this"?

What you say to yourself is often self-prophesizing. Tell yourself that you are on the road to healing and every day you will get closer to that goal. Continually tell yourself that you will never stop grieving and you will carry around your suffering forever.

What are you telling yourself about your loss?

all that is left

*Humor prevents one from becoming a tragic figure
even though he/she is involved in tragic events.*
    –E. T. "Cy" Eberhart, American hospital chaplain

When I was a volunteer with hospice, I would see patients who could not do any of the things that once came so easily to them. They had trouble eating, bathing, and dressing themselves. Everything was taken from them. Sometimes all they had left was their sense of humor.

The same is often true when one has experienced a loss. In her book *Laugh Your Way to Grace*, author Susan Sparks writes about speaking to a woman who lost her husband on 9/11. In describing him in detail for a missing person's report, the woman said, "Oh, I forgot to tell you, he left the house with the worst tie on! It was like this horrible green color with flamingos and palm trees."

Realizing what she just said, the woman started to laugh. After a moment of silence, the woman told Sparks, "You must think me crazy laughing like this." After the pause, the woman whispered, "But laughter is all my family and I have left."

If that is all you feel you have left, then laugh…and make it loud and long.

anesthesia for the heart

Cartoons and humor are not for the good times.
They're for all the bad frustrations, annoyances,
and things bordering on the horrible that happen
to us. And they're even for the horrible things
[that] happen to other people — it's a certain little
anesthesia of the heart which is necessary.
—Bob Mankoff, cartoon editor of the New Yorker

Humor is all around us. Every day there are opportunities to laugh about something.

Take some time today and find one thing — just one thing that amuses you and makes you laugh, even for a short while. It will provide some anesthesia for your heart.

If all you can do is smile loudly, that's okay too.

god-given laughter

Laughter is the God in us.
   —C. McNair Wilson, American author

It has been said that God never gives you more than you can handle. It is also true that God has given you a tool to help you handle what is given to you. That tool is your sense of humor and laughter.

And if you don't think God has a playful sense of humor, consider:

   —the platypus
   —the giraffe
   —the hippopotamus

just laugh

*Even if there is nothing to
laugh about, laugh on credit.*

—Anonymous

Participants in laughter clubs, which started in India, get together on a regular basis to laugh. There are no jokes told, no funny stories shared — only people laughing. They don't have a reason to laugh. They just do it.

You can do it too.

humor and hope

I have seen what a laugh can do.
It can transform almost unbearable
tears into something bearable, even hopeful.
                    —Bob Hope, American comedian

Hope is the greatest treasure you have.

When all else fails, hope is something to hang on to.

Don't give up.

And there is a strong connection between humor, hope, and laughter. When you can find something to laugh about, you are saying that there is hope for the future.

Laughter implies that you can go on.

Laughter implies that you will go on.

If you can find something to laugh about, even for just a few seconds, it is a sign that you can survive your situation.

If you can laugh for a moment,
you can laugh for a moment more,
and a moment after that one too.

additional thoughts on laughing

*You can just as easily laugh and play while you
grow as become serious and overwhelmed.*
—Gary Zukav, American author

*To become conscious of what is
horrifying and to laugh at it is to
become master of that which is horrifying.*
—Eugene Ionesco, Romanian/French playwright

*A sense of humor can help you
overlook the unattractive, tolerate
the unpleasant, cope with the unexpected,
and smile through the unbearable.*
—Moshe Waldoks, American spiritual teacher

closing diary

Sunday, April 13

It is the day of Bernice's unveiling. (In the Jewish tradition, an unveiling is a graveside ceremony within a year of a person's death. It dedicates the grave marker and gives those in mourning a chance to once more honor the deceased.)

It is a somewhat chilly and blustery day in New Jersey. But we are thankful that the forecasted heavy rain did not materialize. We gather around Bernice's low footstone that is covered by a cloth held down with a small stone at each corner.

The service starts with the traditional blessings by the Rabbi. Then, friends and family add their eulogies. Some go on much too long. A number of those gathered seem anxious for the service to conclude. Several times, a strong wind comes up and nearly blows the cloth away.

When this happens, those gathered around look at each other with a slight grin. All probably thinking a similar thought — Bernice's spirit is telling us that it is time to end the service. We could almost hear her saying, "Stop mourning me. Like the wind blowing the cloth away, it is time to move on. It is time to get on with life."

suggested reading

There are lots of books on dealing with both loss and the meaning of life. Some of my favorites are:

Bach, Richard. <u>Illusions</u>. New York: Dell Publishing, 1979.

Broyard, Anatole. <u>Intoxicated by My Illness</u>. New York: Fawcett Columbine, 1992.

Canfield, Jack, et al. <u>Chicken Soup for the Grieving Soul</u>. Deerfield Beach, FL: Health Communications, 1993.

Canfield, Jack, et al. <u>Chicken Soup for the Surviving Soul</u>. Deerfield Beach, FL: Health Communications, 1996.

Carlton, Richard. <u>Don't Sweat the Small Stuff...and it's all small stuff</u>. New York: Hyperion, 1997.

Colgrove, Melba, et. al. <u>How to Survive the Loss of a Love</u>. New York: Leo Press, 1976

Grollman, Earl. When Your Loved One is Dying. Boston: Beacon Press, 1980.

Klein, Allen. The Healing Power of Humor. Los Angeles: J. P. Tarcher, 1989.

Klein, Allen. The Courage to Laugh. Los Angeles: New York: J.P. Tarcher/Putnam, 1998.

Kushner, Harold S. When Bad Things Happen to Good People. New York: Schocken Books, 1981.

Levine, Stephen. Who Dies? Garden City, NY: Anchor Press/Doubleday, 1982.

Prather, Hugh. Notes to Myself. Moab, UT: Real People Press, 1970.

Tatelbaum, Judy. The Courage to Grieve. New York: Lippincott & Crowell, 1980.

Welshons, John. Awakening from Grief. Little Falls, NJ: Open Heart Publications, 2000.

Wilder, Thornton. Our Town: A Play in Three Acts. New York: Coward-McCann, in cooperation with S. French, 1965.

about the author

Allen Klein is a former director of The Life-Death Transitions Institute in San Francisco. Currently he is an award-winning professional speaker and best-selling author. Klein is a recipient of a Lifetime Achievement Award from the Association for Applied and Therapeutic Humor, a Certified Speaking Professional designation from the National Speakers Association, a Communication and Leadership Award from Toastmasters International, and he is an inductee in the Hunter College, New York City, Hall of Fame.

Klein is also the author of 16 books including *The Healing Power of Humor*, *The Courage to Laugh*, and *Change Your Life!: A Little Book of Big Ideas*.

For more information about Klein's books or presentations, go to www.allenklein.com or contact him at: humor@allenklein.com